D0620235
WW
kitchen
collection
Bakes

Gluten-free herby focaccia, page 110

Spinach, walnut & feta rolls, page 38

Baked vanilla cheesecake, page 78

Citrus upside-down cake, page 48

WW
kitchen
collection
Bakes

EGGS We use medium eggs, unless otherwise stated. Pregnant women, the elderly and children should avoid recipes with eggs which are raw or not fully cooked if not produced under the British Lion code of practice.

FRUIT AND VEGETABLES Recipes use medium-size fruit and veg, unless otherwise stated.

LIGHT SOFT CHEESE Where a recipe uses reduced-fat soft cheese, we mean a soft cheese with 30% less fat than its full-fat equivalent.

LOW-FAT SPREAD When a recipe uses a low-fat spread, we mean a spread with a fat content of no more than 39%.

MICROWAVES If we have used a microwave in any of our recipes, the timings will be for an 850-watt microwave oven.

PREP AND COOK TIMES These are approximate and meant to be guidelines only. Prep time includes all steps up to and following the main cooking time(s). Stated cook times may vary according to your oven.

VEGETARIAN ITALIAN-STYLE HARD CHEESE Where we reference this in vegetarian recipes, we mean a cheese similar to Parmesan (which is not vegetarian) but which is suitable for vegetarians.

GLUTEN FREE Recipes displaying the gluten free icon include ingredients that naturally do not contain gluten, but may also contain processed products, such as sauces, stock cubes and spice mixes. If so, you should ensure that those products do not include any gluten-containing ingredients (wheat, barley or rye) – these will be highlighted in the ingredients list on the product's label. Manufacturers may also indicate whether there is a chance that their product may have been accidentally contaminated with gluten during the manufacturing process. For more information and guidance on gluten-free products, visit www.coeliac.org.uk

SMARTPOINTS® have been calculated using the values for generic foods, not brands (except where stated). Tracking using branded items may affect the recorded SmartPoints.

Produced by SevenC3 on behalf of Weight Watchers International, Inc. Published February 2018.

First published in Great Britain by Seven Publishing Ltd.

Seven Publishing Ltd, 3-7 Herbal Hill, London EC1R 5EJ
www.seven.co.uk

10 9 8 7 6 5 4 3 2 1

A CIP catalogue record for this book is available from the British Library.
ISBN: 978-0-9935835-9-9

WEIGHT WATCHERS PUBLICATIONS TEAM
Samantha Rees, Nicola Kirk, Nicola Hill, Stephanie Williams, Ruby Bamford

FOR SEVEN PUBLISHING LTD
FOOD
Food editor Sarah Akhurst
Food assistants Linzi Brechin, Nadine Brown
Nutritionist Alexandra Harris

EDITORIAL
Editor-in-Chief Helen Renshaw
Editor Ward Hellewell
Sub-editors Christine Faughlin, Chloe Hay

DESIGN & PHOTOGRAPHY
Art director Liz Baird
Photography Ant Duncan
Food stylist Sarah Cook
Prop stylist Davina Perkins

ACCOUNT MANAGEMENT
Account manager Gina Cavaciuti
Group publishing director Kirsten Price

PRODUCTION
Production director Sophie Dillon
Colour reproduction by F1 Colour
Printed in the UK by CPI Colour

Contents

There's nothing quite like the smell of a freshly baked loaf or batch of biscuits, and sharing them with family and friends is part of the *pleasure*. If you think following Weight Watchers means you have to hang up your apron and put away your cookie cutters, think again. In this book, we've brought together some delicious *recipes* for you to make and *enjoy*. We've made tweaks to traditional recipes to reduce the SmartPoints values and we've also created recipes using ingredients you may not think of when it comes to baking – the results are *amazing*. There's a range of bakes to try, with the SmartPoints included to help you fit them into everyday life, whether that be tea with friends or a *special* occasion. So what are you waiting for – let's get baking!

WHEN YOU SEE THESE SYMBOLS:

0 SmartPoints value — Tells you how many SmartPoints are in the recipe.

* Indicates a recipe is suitable for freezing.

GF Indicates a recipe is gluten free (see page 6).

V Indicates a recipe is vegetarian.

Top tips

FOR BETTER BAKING

By getting creative with ingredients, you can make biscuits, cakes and pastries that taste amazing and won't scupper your healthy eating plan. Here's how...

LOW-FAT SPREAD

Using unsaturated vegetable-based spreads instead of butter not only helps reduce the SmartPoints, it will also help give your cakes a lighter, fluffier texture.

DARK CHOCOLATE

Good-quality dark chocolate contains less sugar than cheaper, more processed varieties and will give bakes a much richer, more chocolatey flavour. You'll need less of it too. Look for chocolate with at least 70% cocoa solids.

WHOLEMEAL FLOUR

Wholemeal flour gives bakes a slightly denser texture, but it also increases their fibre content and adds a nutty flavour. Try using it in oaty biscuits or fruity cakes – or try using a blend of white and wholemeal flour, to keep the texture light.

FLAVOUR BOOSTERS

Adding plenty of interesting flavours to your bakes means you can reduce the sugar without missing it. Lemon or orange zest, almond and vanilla extracts and spices such as ginger, cinnamon and nutmeg are all great for baking, but why not try others, like coffee, green tea (matcha) or cardamom.

FRUIT & VEGETABLE PUREES

Fruit or veg add sweetness to your cakes and bakes and mean you can use less fat, but still have a rich, moist texture. Apples, pears, bananas, carrots, beetroot, squash and sweet potato all work well. Most can be grated and used raw or cooked and puréed.

FILO PASTRY

Unlike other pastries, filo doesn't contain any fat – oil or butter is usually brushed onto it before baking. Just a light misting of cooking spray will do the trick too and help filo pastry turn golden and crispy, so it's a great substitute for richer puff pastry.

HONEY

Although honey is a form of sugar, it contains more nutrients and is actually sweeter than granulated sugar, so you can use less of it to get the same results. An extra benefit is that it adds a fragrant flavour to your bakes.

0% FAT GREEK YOGURT

Creamy fillings and toppings may taste good, but they'll also add to the SmartPoints in a big way. Instead, use 0% fat natural Greek yogurt – its thick, creamy texture makes it a great substitute for whipped cream in recipes such as pavlovas or roulades.

BEANS

It may sound odd, but tinned beans and pulses make a great substitute for flour and will reduce the SmartPoints (tinned beans in water are a zero Points food). Used in cakes, they'll give a moist texture and you won't notice any difference in flavour. Don't believe us? Give it a try!

OATS

Substituting oats for some of the flour is another way to increase the nutrition factor of your bakes, and they'll also add a nice nuttiness too. Try swapping a quarter of the flour in a recipe for porridge oats.

A FEAST FOR THE EYES

Part of the joy of baking is adding the finishing touches so your creations look as good as they taste. Here are some ways to add appeal without increasing the SmartPoints.

SMALL BUT BEAUTIFUL

Going bite-size means you can still enjoy your favourite bakes, but in more realistic portions. Not only that, making things mini somehow makes them look even more appealing. Try our Rocky road bites, p30.

ICING ON THE CAKE

Sickly sweet icings and thick buttercreams could break your SmartPoints budget and leave you feeling overloaded with sugar. Opt instead for a thin glacé icing or melt chocolate and drizzle it, rather than applying it in a thick layer. Try our Chocolate black bean cake, p60.

JUST A DUSTING

Want to forgo the icing altogether but still make biscuits and cakes look gorgeous? All you need is a light dusting of icing sugar or cocoa powder. Put it in a small sieve to get an even coating. Try our Choc-chip courgette brownies, p20.

AND A CHERRY ON TOP

Fresh fruit will take your bakes from ordinary to awesome. Take advantage it's 0 SmartPoints, so you can go to town. Try the Baked vanilla cheesecake, p78.

CRUMBS!

Here's a neat trick for decorating cakes – take a little bit of the cake, grate it into crumbs and sprinkle them over a thin icing for extra wow factor without any extra ingredients or SmartPoints. Try the Red velvet cupcakes, p56.

SHAPE UP

Think outside the square (or circle) and give your bakes extra appeal by making them in unusual shapes. Look out for fancy cake tins or biscuit cutters and let your imagination run free. Try making our Shortbread biscuits as petticoat tails, p26, rather than the usual rounds.

GO NAKED

Open-topped pies and tarts not only mean you use less pastry, but you also get to see all that lovely filling. Try the Lemon meringue tartlets, p34. If you want a pastry top, go for a lattice, rather than a full covering, and you'll get the best of both worlds.

CUSTOMISE YOUR TOPPINGS

There's nothing wrong with going a bit over the top for a special occasion, but why not make those extra toppings removable, so you don't have to eat them if you don't want to use more SmartPoints. The meringues on our Vanilla cake with meringue kisses, p84, look amazing but can be taken off, saving 2 SmartPoints per serving.

Biscuits, traybakes & pastry

GINGERBREAD BISCOTTI

These twice-baked biscuits are the perfect accompaniment to an after-dinner coffee.

MAKES 16

PREP TIME 20 minutes + cooling **COOK TIME** 50 minutes

INGREDIENTS

170g plain flour, plus extra for dusting
60g dark brown soft sugar
1 teaspoon ground ginger
1 teaspoon ground cinnamon
Pinch of grated nutmeg
1 teaspoon baking powder
¼ teaspoon bicarbonate of soda
50g dried cranberries
35g pistachio kernels
2 eggs, lightly beaten
1 tablespoon treacle

SmartPoints
3 per biscotti

METHOD

1 Preheat the oven to 180°C, fan 160°C, gas mark 4. Line a baking sheet with baking paper.

2 Put the flour, sugar, spices, baking powder, bicarbonate of soda, cranberries and pistachios in a large mixing bowl and stir to combine.

3 Add the eggs and treacle, then mix well until the mixture comes together to a sticky dough.

4 Dust your work surface with the extra flour and turn out the dough. Knead gently for 1 minute, then divide in half. Shape each piece of dough into a 12cm-long log. Transfer both to the prepared baking sheet, leaving space between them, and bake for 30 minutes until firm.

5 Remove from the oven and set aside to cool for 10 minutes. Transfer to a board and cut each log into 8 equal slices. Lay the slices on the baking sheet and bake for another 20 minutes, or until the biscotti are crisp and hard. Cool on a wire rack, then serve.

MARSHMALLOW SQUARES

Get the kids to help out with these easy, no-bake treats that use only three ingredients.

MAKES 16

PREP TIME 10 minutes + chilling **COOK TIME** 10 minutes

INGREDIENTS

50g low-fat spread
165g Weight Watchers mini marshmallows
65g puffed rice

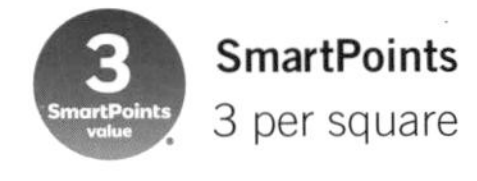

SmartPoints
3 per square

GF See page 6

METHOD

1 Line a 20cm square cake tin with baking paper, leaving some paper hanging over the edge of the tin to make it easy to lift out.

2 In a large pan, melt the low-fat spread over a low heat. Add 150g of the marshmallows and cook over a low heat for about 10 minutes, stirring often, until the marshmallows have melted and the mixture is smooth and combined.

3 Remove from the heat and stir in the puffed rice, mixing well so it is completely coated in the marshmallow mixture.

4 While the mixture is still warm, spoon it into the prepared tin and press lightly with a spatula to smooth the top. Scatter over the remaining marshmallows, then chill for at least 30 minutes to set. Lift out of the tin onto a chopping board and remove the baking paper, then cut into 16 squares and serve.

CHOCOLATE OATY DIGESTIVES

Milk, white or dark chocolate – use whatever you fancy to coat these crisp oat biscuits.

MAKES 12

PREP TIME 15 minutes + cooling **COOK TIME** 15 minutes

INGREDIENTS

40g low-fat spread
40g caster sugar
1 egg
½ teaspoon ground ginger
50g wholemeal flour
65g porridge oats
1 teaspoon baking powder
50g chocolate

SmartPoints
3 per biscuit

METHOD

1 Preheat the oven to 180°C, fan 160°C, gas mark 4. Line a baking sheet with baking paper.

2 In a large mixing bowl, cream together the low-fat spread and sugar using a hand-held electric whisk or wooden spoon. Beat in the egg, a little at a time, until well combined.

3 In a separate bowl, combine the ginger, flour, oats and baking powder. Make a well in the centre and add the spread and egg mixture, then gently stir together – taking care not to overmix.

4 Spoon 12 walnut-size balls of the mixture onto the prepared baking sheet, leaving space between them to spread out, then flatten slightly with the back of the spoon. Bake for 12-15 minutes until golden brown. Allow to cool slightly, then transfer to a wire rack to cool completely.

5 When the biscuits have cooled, melt the chocolate in a heatproof bowl set over a pan of boiling water, or in the microwave. Dip one half of each biscuit in the melted chocolate, then return to the wire rack to set.

CHOC-CHIP COURGETTE BROWNIES

These decadent, chocolatey treats contain grated courgette, although you'd never know it!

MAKES 20

PREP TIME 30 minutes **COOK TIME** 1 hour 25 minutes

INGREDIENTS

175g low-fat spread, cut into cubes, plus extra for greasing
150g dark chocolate, roughly chopped
3 eggs
175g caster sugar
150g wholemeal self-raising flour
275g grated courgette (about 1 large courgette)
1 teaspoon cocoa powder

SmartPoints
6 per brownie

METHOD

1 Preheat the oven to 180°C, fan 160°C, gas mark 4. Grease a 20cm square tin with low-fat spread and line with baking paper, leaving some paper hanging over the edge of the tin to make it easy to lift out.

2 Put the chocolate and low-fat spread in a heatproof bowl set over a pan of gently boiling water, making sure the water isn't high enough to touch the bowl. Stir occasionally until the chocolate and spread have melted, then remove from the heat and set aside.

3 In a separate bowl, whisk the eggs and sugar together using a hand-held electric whisk for a few minutes until thick. Pour in the melted chocolate and spread, then fold together until combined. Gently fold in the flour, followed by the grated courgette.

4 Pour the mixture into the prepared tin and smooth the top with a spatula. Bake for 1 hour 15 minutes, until only a few crumbs remain when you insert a skewer into the centre of the brownie.

5 Remove from the oven and put the tin on a wire rack. Leave until completely cool, then use the baking paper to lift the brownie out of the tin. Remove the baking paper, dust the top with the cocoa powder and cut into 20 individual brownies.

BANANA, OAT & RAISIN BISCUITS

Fill up the cookie jar with these easy, gluten-free biscuits, ready in less than half an hour.

MAKES 18

PREP TIME 10 minutes **COOK TIME** 15 minutes

INGREDIENTS

4 ripe bananas, mashed
125g porridge oats
75g raisins

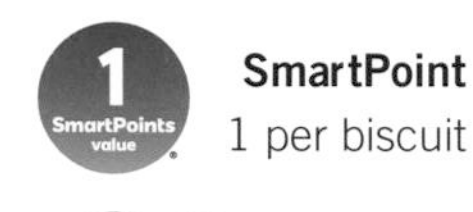

SmartPoint
1 per biscuit

V GF See page 6

METHOD

1 Preheat the oven to 180°C, fan 160°C, gas mark 4 and line 2 baking sheets with baking paper.

2 Put the bananas in a large bowl and stir in the oats and raisins until well combined.

3 Drop spoonfuls of the mixture onto the prepared baking sheets to make 18 biscuits. Bake for 12-15 minutes or until cooked through and golden. Cool on a wire rack, then serve.

Tip

Want to spice these up? Add 1 teaspoon ground ginger or cinnamon to the mixture for no extra SmartPoints.

Banana,
oat & raisin
biscuits

RASPBERRY & COCONUT SLICES

This traditional-style bake combines fresh raspberries and coconut – a flavour match made in heaven!

MAKES 16

PREP TIME 15 minutes + cooling **COOK TIME** 30 minutes

INGREDIENTS

130g low-fat spread, plus extra for greasing
200g plain flour
60g caster sugar
50g porridge oats
40g desiccated coconut
Pinch of salt
250g raspberries

SmartPoints
4 per slice

METHOD

1 Preheat the oven to 190°C, fan 170°C, gas mark 5. Grease a 22cm square cake tin and line with baking paper.

2 In a large mixing bowl, combine the flour, sugar, oats and coconut with a pinch of salt. Add the spread and rub it into the dry ingredients with your fingertips until combined and the mixture resembles coarse crumbs.

3 Press half the mixture into the prepared tin. Top with the raspberries, pressing down gently with a spatula to release some of the juice. Scatter over the remaining oat mixture and smooth with a spatula – it doesn't matter if some of the raspberries are peeking through.

4 Bake for 30 minutes or until golden brown. Remove from the oven and set aside to cool in the tin for 1 hour, then turn out onto a chopping board and remove the baking paper. Cut into 16 squares and serve.

SHORTBREAD BISCUITS

These pretty shortbread 'petticoat tails' make a lovely centrepiece for an afternoon tea with friends.

MAKES 32

PREP TIME 20 minutes + chilling **COOK TIME** 15 minutes

INGREDIENTS

175g low-fat spread
75g caster sugar
1 egg
300g plain flour, plus extra for dusting
1 teaspoon baking powder

SmartPoints
2 per biscuit

METHOD

1 In a large mixing bowl, cream together the low-fat spread and sugar using a hand-held electric whisk or wooden spoon, then beat in the egg. Sift in the flour and the baking powder and combine until you have a stiff dough. Using your hands, press together into a ball, then wrap in clingfilm and chill in the freezer for 30 minutes to firm up.

2 Preheat the oven to 190°C, fan 170°C, gas mark 5.

3 Cut the dough in half. Put a piece of baking paper onto your work surface and dust with a little flour, then roll out one portion of the dough into a 22cm round on the baking paper. Using a fork, pierce the dough to mark out 16 equal segments – it helps if you mark it out in quarters first, then mark out each quarter into 4 more segments. Crimp the edge of the pastry round with your fingers, then lift the baking paper and dough onto a baking sheet.

4 Repeat with the remaining dough and place on a second baking sheet, then bake both rounds for 15 minutes, or until golden brown. Remove from the oven and transfer to a wire rack to cool. Cut into segments to serve.

Tip

If you don't want to make petticoats, use a square biscuit cutter to cut out 32 biscuits from the dough. You may need to reroll the trimmings.

WHITE CHOCOLATE BLONDIES

There's a secret ingredient hiding in these white chocolate treats – zero hero chickpeas!

MAKES 18

PREP TIME 20 minutes + cooling **COOK TIME** 40 minutes

INGREDIENTS

60g low-fat spread, plus extra for greasing
400g tin chickpeas, drained and rinsed
3 eggs
1½ teaspoons almond extract
50g granulated sugar
75g dark brown soft sugar
1 teaspoon baking powder
65g ground almonds
90g white chocolate chips

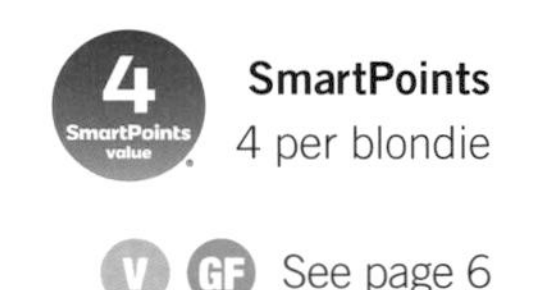

SmartPoints
4 per blondie

See page 6

METHOD

1 Preheat the oven to 180°C, fan 160°C, gas mark 4. Grease a 25cm square cake tin with low-fat spread and line with baking paper.

2 Put the chickpeas and low-fat spread in a food processor with one of the eggs and blend to a purée. Transfer to a bowl and stir in the almond extract.

3 In a separate bowl, beat the remaining eggs with both sugars using a hand-held electric whisk. Fold the mixture into the chickpea purée. Add the baking powder and ground almonds and fold to combine. Stir 70g of the white chocolate chips through the mixture.

4 Pour the mixture into the tin and smooth the top with a spatula. Bake for 35-40 minutes, or until the top is golden brown and firm, and a skewer inserted into the middle of the blondie comes out clean. Remove from the oven and leave to cool in the tin for 15 minutes. Turn out onto a wire rack, remove the baking paper and leave to cool completely.

5 Melt the remaining chocolate chips in a microwave for around 30 seconds. Using a teaspoon, drizzle the melted chocolate over the blondies. Leave to set, then cut into 18 bars.

ROCKY ROAD BITES

Everyone loves these easy, no-bake bites – the perfect size for when you want just a little sweet treat.

MAKES 20

PREP TIME 10 minutes + cooling & chilling **COOK TIME** 1 minute

INGREDIENTS

50g low-fat spread
150g dark chocolate, broken into pieces
50g Weight Watchers mini marshmallows
70g reduced-fat rich tea biscuits, crushed into small pieces

SmartPoints
3 per bite

METHOD

1 Line an 18cm square cake tin with baking paper, leaving some paper hanging over the edge of the tin to make it easy to lift out. Put the low-fat spread and chocolate in a large microwave-safe bowl and heat in the microwave for 1 minute, or until melted. Set aside for 5 minutes to cool slightly.

2 Reserve a few of the marshmallows for decoration, then add the rest to the chocolate mixture, along with the biscuits, and stir well to combine. Spoon the mixture in the prepared tin and smooth the top with a spatula. Scatter over the reserved marshmallows and chill for 1 hour or until set.

3 Lift the rocky road out of the tin, remove the baking paper and cut into 20 equal pieces.

CARROT CAKE FLAPJACKS

This simple recipe combines carrot cake with flapjacks to give you the best of both worlds!

MAKES 20

PREP TIME 15 minutes + cooling **COOK TIME** 25 minutes

INGREDIENTS

100g low-fat spread
3 tablespoons golden syrup
225g porridge oats
2 eggs, beaten
2 carrots, grated
40g sultanas
Grated zest of 1 orange
1½ teaspoons mixed spice

SmartPoints
3 per flapjack

V GF See page 6

METHOD

1 Preheat the oven to 180°C, fan 160°C, gas mark 4. Melt the spread in a large pan over a low heat. Brush a little of the melted spread over the base and sides of a 30cm x 20cm swiss roll tin, then line the base with baking paper.

2 Stir the golden syrup into the melted spread, then add the oats, eggs, carrots, sultanas, orange zest and mixed spice. Stir well until everything is combined.

3 Put the mixture into the prepared tin and smooth the surface with a spatula. Bake for 20 minutes until firm and golden. Cool in the tin for 30 minutes, then turn out onto a chopping board, remove the baking paper and cut into 20 pieces to serve.

LEMON MERINGUE TARTLETS

The classic dessert in miniature form is made easy with Weight Watchers ready-made meringues.

MAKES 24

PREP TIME 30 minutes **COOK TIME** 20 minutes

INGREDIENTS

200g reduced-fat shortcrust pastry
3 lemons
20g cornflour
80g caster sugar
30g low-fat spread
2 egg yolks
24 Weight Watchers mini meringues

SmartPoints
2 per tartlet

METHOD

1 Preheat the oven to 200°C, fan 180°C, gas mark 6. Roll out the pastry and cut out 24 discs with a 6cm round cutter – you may need to reroll the trimmings. Use the pastry to line a 24-hole a mini pie tin.

2 Cut 24 small squares of baking paper and put a few baking beans in the middle of each piece. Scrunch the paper around the beans and put them in the pastry cases, then bake for 10-15 minutes. Remove the baking paper and beans and return to the oven to cook for a further 5 minutes, or until golden brown. Remove from the oven and leave to cool slightly. Transfer to a wire rack and leave to cool completely.

3 Meanwhile, grate the zest from 2 of the lemons and squeeze the juice from all 3. Put the cornflour, lemon zest, juice, and sugar in a pan with 4 tablespoons water. Heat over a gentle heat, stirring continuously, until the mixture comes to a boil and starts to thicken. Remove from the heat and whisk in the low-fat spread and egg yolks. Leave to cool slightly. Divide the mixture between the pastry tart cases and leave to cool completely.

4 Top each lemon tart with a mini meringue, then serve.

MINI PLUM TURNOVERS

Using ready-rolled pastry makes these fruity treats simple to make. Serve warm as a dessert, or cold for teatime.

MAKES 12

PREP TIME 20 minutes + cooling **COOK TIME** 20 minutes

INGREDIENTS

250g plums, stones removed and roughly chopped
1 star anise
1 cinnamon stick
1 tablespoon agave syrup
375g ready-rolled reduced-fat puff pastry (you will have 60g of offcuts)
1 egg, beaten
2 teaspoons icing sugar

SmartPoints
3 per turnover

METHOD

1 Put the plums in a pan with the star anise, cinnamon and agave syrup. Cover and cook over a low heat for 5 minutes, until the plums start to soften. Remove the lid and continue to cook until sticky. Remove from the heat and set aside to cool, then discard the star anise and cinnamon stick.

2 Preheat the oven to 200°C, fan 180°C, gas mark 6 and line a baking sheet with baking paper. Unroll the pastry on your work surface and cut into 12 x 8cm squares, discarding the trimmings. Put a spoonful of the spiced plum mixture on one corner of each square, then brush a little of the beaten egg around the edges. Fold over one corner to create a triangle and press with your fingers to seal the edges.

3 Put the turnovers on the prepared baking sheet and brush with the remaining egg. Bake for 15 minutes, or until crisp and golden. Leave to cool for 10 minutes, then serve dusted with icing sugar.

SPINACH, WALNUT & FETA ROLLS

These vegetarian rolls are a great addition to an afternoon tea, or perfect for a light lunch.

MAKES 8

PREP TIME 20 minutes + cooling **COOK TIME** 30 minutes

INGREDIENTS

Calorie controlled cooking spray
1 large onion, finely chopped
200g young leaf spinach
100g light feta, crumbled
25g walnut halves, finely chopped
40g fresh breadcrumbs
2 large sheets filo pastry (25cm x 45cm)
½ teaspoon sesame seeds

SmartPoints
3 per roll

METHOD

1 Mist a large frying pan with cooking spray and cook the onion for 6-8 minutes over a medium heat until softened, adding a splash of water if needed to stop it catching. Add the spinach and cook until it has wilted and any excess moisture has evaporated. Transfer to a plate and spread out to cool, then squeeze out any excess liquid. Transfer to a bowl and mix in the feta, walnuts and breadcrumbs, then season to taste.

2 Preheat the oven to 220°C, fan 200°C, gas mark 7 and line a baking sheet with baking paper. Mist the tops of both sheets of filo with cooking spray, then lay one on top of the other. Spoon the filling along one long side of the pastry, then roll up like a sausage roll.

3 With the pastry seam underneath, make a few cuts through the top of the filo to expose the filling, then slice the roll into 8 equal pieces. Mist the tops with a little more cooking spray and scatter over the sesame seeds. Put on the prepared baking sheet and bake for 20 minutes or until the pastry is crisp and golden, then serve.

BUTTERNUT SQUASH GALETTE

This easy savoury tart is filled with creamy ricotta, red onions and butternut squash.

SERVES 6

PREP TIME 30 minutes + chilling **COOK TIME** 1 hour

INGREDIENTS

200g plain flour
75g low-fat spread
Pinch of salt
1 egg yolk, plus
1 whole egg, beaten
1 large butternut squash, peeled, deseeded and cut into 2cm cubes
4 red onions, cut into wedges
2 garlic cloves, unpeeled
1 tablespoon olive oil
3 sprigs fresh rosemary, leaves picked and finely chopped
125g ricotta

SmartPoints
7 per serving

METHOD

1 Put the flour in a food processor with the spread and a pinch of salt. Pulse until the mixture resembles breadcrumbs. Add the egg yolk and 1 tablespoon cold water and pulse again until the pastry starts to come together into a ball. If the pastry is not coming together, add a splash of cold water. Remove from the processor and gently knead into a disc. Wrap in clingfilm and chill in the fridge for 30 minutes.

2 Preheat the oven to 200°C, fan 180°C, gas mark 6 and line a baking sheet with baking paper. Put the butternut squash in a roasting tin with the onions and garlic. Drizzle over the oil and season to taste. Roast for 30-35 minutes, or until tender. Remove from the oven and squeeze out the garlic flesh from the skin. Stir the garlic through the vegetables, then set aside.

3 Roll out the pastry into a large circle, about the size of a large dinner plate, and put on the prepared baking sheet. Pile the squash and onion mixture in the middle of the pastry, leaving a 4cm border. Scatter over the rosemary and the ricotta. Gently fold the edges of the pastry up around the filling, leaving the top of the galette open. Brush the pastry edges with the beaten egg and bake for 25 minutes, or until the pastry is golden brown. Serve warm or cold.

SLOW-ROASTED TOMATO TART

Enjoy the classic Italian flavours of this tasty tart that can be eaten warm or cold.

SERVES 6

PREP TIME 20 minutes **COOK TIME** 1 hour 30 minutes

INGREDIENTS

800g mixed tomatoes (we used golden cherry, baby plum and vine tomatoes), halved or quartered if large
1 teaspoon olive oil
1 tablespoon balsamic vinegar
Pinch of chilli flakes
375g ready-rolled reduced-fat puff pastry (you will have 35g of offcuts)
125g light mozzarella, very thinly sliced
Handful fresh basil leaves

SmartPoints
8 per serving

METHOD

1 Preheat the oven to 160°C, fan 140°C, gas mark 3. Put the tomatoes in a large roasting tin and drizzle over the oil and vinegar, then scatter over the chilli flakes. Season to taste and roast for 1 hour, until the tomatoes are starting to dehydrate. Remove from the oven and set aside.

2 Increase the oven temperature to 200°C, fan 180°C, gas mark 6 and line a baking sheet with baking paper. Unroll the pastry and trim the edges to a 20cm x 30cm rectangle, discarding the trimmings. Put the pastry on the prepared baking sheet and score a 1.5cm border. Prick the inner rectangle all over with a fork. Bake for 15 minutes, until the pastry has risen and is starting to turn golden.

3 Remove from the oven and arrange the tomatoes on the inner rectangle, leaving the border uncovered. Top the tomatoes with the mozzarella and return to the oven for another 10-12 minutes, or until the mozzarella is melted and golden. Remove from the oven and scatter over the basil leaves to serve.

TOFFEE APPLE PIE

A healthier, quicker version of a traditional apple pie that makes a great dessert for Sunday lunch.

SERVES 4

PREP TIME 20 minutes **COOK TIME** 40 minutes

INGREDIENTS

8 eating apples peeled, cored and sliced
½ teaspoon ground cinnamon
3 tablespoons toffee sauce
40g low-fat spread
3 large sheets of filo pastry (25cm x 45cm)
4 tablespoons 0% fat natural Greek yogurt, to serve

SmartPoints
6 per serving

METHOD

1 Put the apples and cinnamon in a pan with 75ml water. Cook over a medium heat for 15 minutes, or until all the water has evaporated and the apples are tender. Transfer to a small round pie dish and drizzle over the toffee sauce.

2 Preheat the oven to 190°C, fan 170°C, gas mark 5.

3 Melt the low-fat spread in a small pan over a low heat. Lay one of the filo sheets on your work surface and brush the top with some of the melted spread. Scrunch it up slightly and place on top of the pie. Repeat with the remaining pastry until the surface of the pie is covered.

4 Bake for 20-25 minutes, or until the pastry is crisp and golden, then serve warm with the Greek yogurt.

Cakes &
desserts

CITRUS UPSIDE-DOWN CAKE

Slices of caramelised orange turn this simple cake into something really special.

SERVES 12

PREP TIME 20 minutes + cooling **COOK TIME** 1 hour

INGREDIENTS

2 oranges
160g caster sugar
1 blood orange, very thinly sliced
160g low-fat spread
3 eggs
1 teaspoon vanilla bean paste or vanilla extract
160g self-raising flour

SmartPoints
6 per serving

METHOD

1 Preheat the oven to 180°C, fan 160°C, gas mark 4. Line a 20cm square cake tin with baking paper.

2 Grate the zest from the 2 oranges, then thinly slice one and squeeze the juice from the other. Put 100g of the sugar in a large frying pan with 50ml water. Heat over a gentle heat, stirring, until the sugar has dissolved. Turn up the heat and add the sliced orange and the blood orange. Simmer for 10-15 minutes, or until the orange slices are soft and the liquid is syrupy. Using a slotted spoon, remove the fruit from the pan and set aside to cool. Stir the orange juice into the liquid in the pan and set aside.

3 In a large mixing bowl, cream together the remaining sugar and the low-fat spread using a hand-held electric whisk. Add the eggs, one at a time, beating between each addition. Add the orange zest and vanilla bean paste or extract and stir well to incorporate. Gently fold in the flour until you have a smooth batter.

4 Arrange the orange slices over the base of the prepared tin, then pour over the cake mixture. Bake for 30-35 minutes, or until golden and a skewer inserted into the centre of the cake comes out clean. Remove from the oven and set aside to cool in the tin.

5 Turn the cake out onto a serving plate and remove the baking paper. Brush the orange syrup over the top of the cake, then slice and serve.

Tip

If you can't find blood oranges, use another regular orange – you won't get the vivid colour, but the flavour will still be great!

RASPBERRY FRIANDS

Using just the whites of the eggs keeps these little cakes lovely and light.

MAKES 10

PREP TIME 15 minutes + cooling **COOK TIME** 25 minutes

INGREDIENTS

Calorie controlled cooking spray
85g low-fat spread
100g icing sugar, plus an extra 1 teaspoon for dusting
75g ground almonds
25g plain flour
3 egg whites
125g raspberries

SmartPoints
5 per friand

METHOD

1 Preheat the oven to 200°C, fan 180°C, gas mark 6. Mist a 12-hole friand or muffin tin with cooking spray.

2 Melt the low-fat spread in a pan over a low heat, then set aside. Put the icing sugar, ground almonds and flour into a large mixing bowl.

3 In a separate bowl, whisk the egg whites until foamy, but not stiff. Make a well in the centre of the dry ingredients and fold in the egg whites and melted spread, until you have a smooth batter.

4 Divide the batter between 10 of the muffin holes and top each friand with 3 raspberries. Bake for 20-25 minutes, or until golden and a skewer inserted into the centre of a friand comes out clean.

5 Remove from the oven and leave to cool for 10 minutes, then turn out of the tin and leave to cool completely on a wire rack. Serve dusted with icing sugar.

TIRAMISU ROULADE

The popular Italian dessert is reinvented as a swiss roll – deliciously light sponge with a coffee flavoured filling.

SERVES 8

PREP TIME 30 minutes + cooling **COOK TIME** 15 minutes

INGREDIENTS

5 egg whites
¼ teaspoon cream of tartar
Pinch of salt
40g plain flour
2 tablespoons cocoa powder, plus an extra 1 teaspoon for dusting
100g caster sugar
1 teaspoon instant coffee granules
½ tablespoon icing sugar
125g quark
1 tablespoon Marsala wine
10g dark chocolate, finely grated

SmartPoints
5 per serving

METHOD

1 Preheat the oven to 180°C, fan 160°C, gas mark 4. Line a 20cm x 30cm swiss roll tin with baking paper.

2 In a large mixing bowl, whisk the egg whites until foamy, then add the cream of tartar with a pinch of salt and continue to whisk until the mixture is stiff and forms peaks that hold their shape when the beaters are removed.

3 Sift the flour, 2 tablespoons cocoa and sugar over the egg white mixture, then gently fold until smooth and combined.

4 Spoon the batter into the prepared tin and smooth the surface with a spatula. Bake for 12-15 minutes or until the sponge feels firm and springy to the touch.

5 Lightly dust a sheet of baking paper with 1 teaspoon cocoa powder. Turn the cake out onto the baking paper, discarding the sheet from the tin, then roll up the roulade from one short side, with the cocoa-dusted paper inside as you roll. Set aside to cool.

6 Put the coffee granules in a mixing bowl, add 1 teaspoon boiling water and stir to dissolve. Add the icing sugar and quark, and mix until smooth and combined.

7 Unroll the sponge and drizzle over the Marsala wine, then spread over the quark mixture. Scatter over half of the grated chocolate and re-roll the sponge without the paper. Scatter the remaining chocolate over the top of the roulade and cut into slices to serve.

CINNAMON APPLE MADELEINES

Apple purée keeps these little cakes nice and moist, and reduces the amount of fat and added sugar.

MAKES 20

PREP TIME 20 minutes + cooling & chilling **COOK TIME** 20 minutes

INGREDIENTS

- **1 small apple, peeled, cored and roughly chopped**
- **½ teaspoon vanilla extract**
- **65g low-fat spread**
- **50g plain flour, plus an extra 1 tablespoon for dusting**
- **1 teaspoon ground cinnamon**
- **½ teaspoon baking powder**
- **1 large egg**
- **3 tablespoons caster sugar**
- **½ teaspoon icing sugar**

YOU WILL ALSO NEED

Madeleine tin

SmartPoints

1 per Madeleine

METHOD

1 Put the apple in a heavy-based pan with 50ml water and the vanilla extract. Cover and cook over a low heat for 6-8 minutes until tender. Purée the apple using a stick blender or mini food processor.

2 Melt the spread in a small pan over a low heat. Brush a 12-hole Madeleine tin with a little of the spread, being sure to get into all the ridges. Dust with the extra tablespoon of flour and shake off any excess. Chill the tin in the fridge while you make the batter.

3 Sift together the remaining flour, cinnamon and baking powder in a small bowl. In a separate bowl, beat the egg using a hand-held electric whisk until thick. Add the caster sugar and continue to beat for about 2 minutes. Add the flour to the egg mixture and gently stir together. Fold in the apple purée and the remaining melted spread, then chill for 30 minutes.

4 Preheat the oven to 190°C, fan 170°C, gas mark 5. Spoon the chilled batter into the prepared Madeleine tin, filling the moulds almost to the top, then bake for 11-12 minutes. Carefully remove the Madeleines from the tin and put on a wire rack to cool, then dust with the icing sugar to serve.

RED VELVET CUPCAKES

With their light, fluffy texture, striking red colour and cream cheese frosting, these are always a favourite.

MAKES 12

PREP TIME 20 minutes + cooling **COOK TIME** 20 minutes

INGREDIENTS

60g low-fat spread
125g caster sugar
1 egg
10g cocoa powder
1 x 15g tube red gel food colouring
1 teaspoon vanilla extract
100ml low-fat natural yogurt
150g plain flour, sifted
½ teaspoon bicarbonate of soda
½ tablespoon white wine vinegar
2 tablespoons skimmed milk

FOR THE FROSTING

150g low-fat soft cheese
75g 0% natural Greek yogurt
1 tablespoon icing sugar
1 teaspoon vanilla extract

SmartPoints
5 per cupcake

METHOD

1 Preheat the oven to 180°C, fan 160°C, gas mark 4. Line a 12-hole muffin tin with paper cases.

2 Put the low-fat spread and caster sugar in a mixing bowl and beat with a hand-held electric whisk until pale and fluffy. Add the egg and continue beating until well combined. Sift in the cocoa powder, add the food colouring and vanilla, and beat until combined.

3 Mix in half the yogurt, followed by half the flour, beating well. Repeat with the rest of the yogurt and flour, and beat for 2 minutes until fluffy. On a low speed, beat in the bicarbonate of soda and white wine vinegar, then add enough milk to get a mixture that drops easily from a spoon.

4 Divide the mixture between the muffin cases and bake for 20 minutes or until the cupcakes are risen and springy to the touch. Cool in the tin for a few minutes, then transfer to a wire rack to cool completely.

5 Use a teaspoon to dig out a small hollow in the centre of each cooled cupcake, and grate the removed pieces of sponge into a bowl, so you have fine red cake crumbs.

6 To make the frosting, mix the soft cheese, yogurt, icing sugar and vanilla in a small bowl. Swirl on top of the cooled cupcakes, filling the hollows, then scatter over the cake crumbs to decorate.

BLUEBERRY YOGURT CAKE

This delicious loaf cake is flavoured with lemon and blueberries, and topped with a blueberry compote.

SERVES 12

PREP TIME 20 minutes + cooling **COOK TIME** 55 minutes

INGREDIENTS

125g low-fat spread
150g caster sugar
3 eggs
100g low-fat natural yogurt
Grated zest of 1 lemon
1 teaspoon vanilla extract
200g self-raising flour
250g blueberries
1 teaspoon icing sugar, to decorate

SmartPoints
6 per serving

METHOD

1 Preheat the oven to 180°C, fan 160°C, gas mark 4. Line a 900g loaf tin with a paper loaf tin liner or baking paper.

2 Put the low-fat spread, caster sugar, eggs, yogurt, lemon zest and vanilla extract in a bowl, and whisk until combined. Gently fold in the flour until you have a smooth batter, then add half the blueberries and stir to combine.

3 Pour the mixture into the prepared loaf tin and bake for 45-50 minutes, or until well risen and a skewer inserted into the centre of the cake comes out clean. Remove from the oven and leave to cool in the tin for 10 minutes, then turn out onto a wire rack and leave to cool completely.

4 Meanwhile, put the remaining blueberries in a pan and cover with a lid. Cook over a low heat for approximately 5 minutes, or until they are soft and have started to release their juice. Set aside to cool.

5 When the cake is completely cool, remove the paper liner and spoon the blueberry compote over the top. Dust with the icing sugar and cut into slices to serve.

CHOCOLATE BLACK BEAN CAKE

This gluten-free chocolate cake uses black beans instead of flour, which helps keep it lovely and moist.

SERVES 10

PREP TIME 20 minutes + cooling **COOK TIME** 45 minutes

INGREDIENTS

- 100g low-fat spread, plus extra for greasing
- 400g tin black beans, drained and rinsed
- 5 eggs
- 2 teaspoons vanilla bean paste or vanilla extract
- 100g light brown soft sugar
- 50g cocoa powder
- 1 teaspoon baking powder
- ½ teaspoon bicarbonate of soda
- 20g white chocolate
- 20g milk chocolate

V GF See page 6

METHOD

1 Preheat the oven to 180°C, fan 160°C, gas mark 4. Grease an 18cm round cake tin with low-fat spread and line with baking paper.

2 Put the black beans, 3 of the eggs and the vanilla bean paste or extract in a food processor and blitz until smooth.

3 In a large mixing bowl, beat together the low-fat spread and sugar using a hand-held electric whisk until pale and fluffy. Add the remaining eggs, one at a time, beating well after each addition. Add the black bean mixture to the bowl and stir until well combined. Finally, gently fold in the cocoa powder, baking powder and bicarbonate of soda until everything is incorporated.

4 Pour the mixture into the prepared tin and bake for 40-45 minutes, or until a skewer inserted into the centre of the cake comes out clean. Remove from the oven and leave to cool in the tin for 15 minutes, then turn out onto a wire rack and leave to cool completely.

5 Put the white and milk chocolate in 2 separate small microwave-safe bowls and microwave each one for 30 seconds until the chocolate has melted. Drizzle over the cake. Leave to set, then serve.

PEAR & CHAI CAKE

Juicy pears top this easy sponge that's flavoured with mixed spices and glazed with maple syrup.

SERVES 12

PREP TIME 20 minutes + cooling **COOK TIME** 30 minutes

INGREDIENTS

- 100g low-fat spread, plus extra for greasing
- 4 ripe Conference pears, peeled, halved and cored
- 6 tablespoons maple syrup, plus an extra 2 teaspoons for glazing
- 3 eggs, beaten
- 100g low-fat yogurt
- 250g plain flour
- 1 teaspoon baking powder
- 1 teaspoon bicarbonate of soda
- 1 teaspoon ground cinnamon
- 1 teaspoon ground ginger
- ½ teaspoon fennel seeds, crushed
- 5 cardamom pods, seeds removed and crushed

SmartPoints
5 per serving

METHOD

1 Preheat the oven to 180°C, fan 160°C, gas mark 4. Grease a 20cm x 30cm baking tin with low-fat spread and line with baking paper.

2 Put one of the pears in a mini processor and blitz to a purée, then set aside.

3 In a large mixing bowl, beat together the low-fat spread and maple syrup using a hand-held electric whisk until smooth and well combined, then whisk in the beaten eggs, yogurt and pear purée.

4 In a separate bowl, mix together all of the dry ingredients, then gently fold them through the spread and egg mixture until you have a smooth batter.

5 Pour the batter into the prepared tin and smooth the top with a spatula, then arrange the remaining 6 pear halves, cut side up, on top. Bake for 25-30 minutes, or until risen and golden and a skewer inserted into the centre of the cake comes out clean.

6 Remove from the oven and brush over the extra maple syrup. Leave to cool in the tin for 15 minutes, then turn out onto a wire rack, remove the baking paper and leave to cool completely before serving.

FIG & GINGER PAVLOVA

Topped with vanilla-flavoured yogurt and roasted figs, this show-stopping dessert is perfect for entertaining.

SERVES 10

PREP TIME 25 minutes + cooling **COOK TIME** 1 hour 25 minutes

INGREDIENTS

8 fresh figs, quartered
2 balls of preserved stem ginger, chopped, plus 1 tablespoon of the ginger syrup
4 egg whites
½ teaspoon cream of tartar
200g golden caster sugar
1 tablespoon icing sugar
1 teaspoon vanilla bean paste or vanilla extract
500g 0% fat natural Greek yogurt

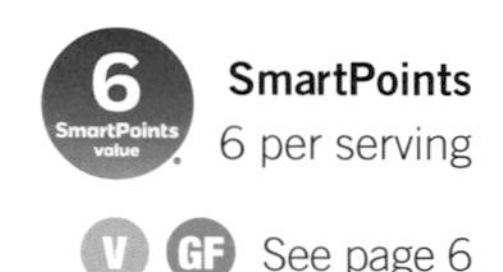

SmartPoints
6 per serving

V GF See page 6

METHOD

1 Preheat the oven to 140°C, fan 120°C, gas mark 1. Line a roasting tin with baking paper. Arrange the figs in the tin, scatter over the chopped ginger and drizzle over the syrup. Cover with kitchen foil and bake for 20-25 minutes, or until sticky. Set aside to cool.

2 Put the egg whites in the bowl of a stand mixer and sprinkle over the cream of tartar. Whisk until the egg whites are stiff and form peaks that hold their shape when the beaters are removed. Gradually add the caster sugar, a tablespoon at a time, whisking thoroughly after each addition, until all the sugar has been incorporated and the mixture is stiff and glossy.

3 Line a baking sheet with baking paper. Spoon the meringue mixture onto the paper, then use a spatula to form a circle the size of a dinner plate, making the sides higher than the middle. Bake for 1 hour, then turn off the oven, leaving the door closed. Leave for at least 3 hours, or overnight, until completely cool. This gradual cooling helps stop the meringue from cracking.

4 Carefully fold the icing sugar and vanilla bean paste or extract through the Greek yogurt. Spoon the mixture into the centre of the meringue, then decorate with the roasted figs and ginger. Chill until you're ready to serve.

CHOCOLATE ANGEL FOOD CAKE

A light-as-a-feather chocolate sponge topped with a soft cheese frosting and fresh strawberries.

SERVES 14

PREP TIME 25 minutes + cooling **COOK TIME** 35 minutes

INGREDIENTS

10 egg whites
1 teaspoon cream of tartar
Pinch of salt
245g icing sugar, sifted
30g cocoa powder
1 teaspoon vanilla bean paste or vanilla extract
90g plain flour
20g cornflour

FOR THE ICING & DECORATION

100g low-fat soft cheese
1 tablespoon cocoa powder, plus an extra ½ teaspoon for dusting
2 tablespoons icing sugar
7 fresh strawberries, halved to decorate

YOU WILL ALSO NEED

25cm angel food tin, chiffon cake tin or bundt tin
Piping bag fitted with a star-shaped nozzle

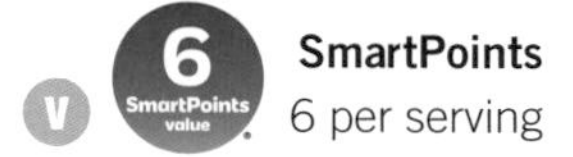

SmartPoints
6 per serving

METHOD

1 Preheat the oven to 170°C, fan 150°C, gas mark 3½. Put the egg whites in the bowl of a freestanding mixer and add the cream of tartar and a pinch of salt. Whisk on medium speed until the egg whites form stiff peaks that hold their shape when the whisk is removed. Add the icing sugar and cocoa powder, a couple of tablespoons at a time, whisking well between each addition.

2 Add the vanilla bean paste or extract and half the flour, and gently fold in using a metal spoon or spatula until the ingredients are well incorporated. Fold in the rest of the flour and the cornflour until you have a smooth batter.

3 Pour the mixture into an ungreased, unlined, loose-bottomed 25cm angel food or chiffon cake tin. If you don't have either of these, use a nonstick bundt cake tin that's been misted with calorie controlled cooking spray. Smooth the surface with a spatula to get rid of any air bubbles. Bake for 30-35 minutes, or until a skewer inserted in the centre of the cake comes out clean.

4 Turn the tin upside down and leave on a wire rack for around 45 minutes to an hour to allow the cake to cool completely. Run a knife around the edges of the cake to release it from the tin.

5 To make the icing, put the soft cheese, cocoa powder and icing sugar in a bowl and whisk together using a hand-held electric whisk. Pipe 14 rosettes of the frosting around the top of the cake and put half a strawberry on each rosette to decorate, then dust with the extra cocoa powder and serve.

ETON MESS ROULADE

A less messy, but just as delicious version of the popular dessert – this can be served in nice neat slices!

SERVES 10

PREP TIME 25 minutes + cooling **COOK TIME** 20 minutes

INGREDIENTS

4 egg whites
225g caster sugar plus an extra 1 tablespoon
½ tablespoon cornflour
1 teaspoon white wine vinegar
200g strawberries, hulled and roughly chopped
350g 0% fat natural Greek yogurt
½ teaspoon icing sugar

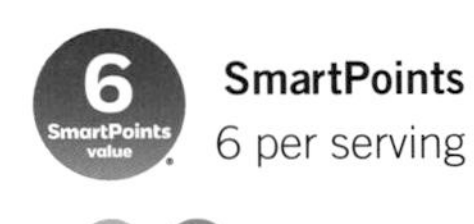

SmartPoints
6 per serving

See page 6

METHOD

1 Preheat the oven to 160°C, fan 140°C, gas mark 3. Line a 25cm x 35cm swiss roll tin with baking paper.

2 In a large mixing bowl, Use a hand-held electric whisk to whisk the egg whites until they form stiff peaks that hold their shape when the beaters are removed. Gradually beat in 225g caster sugar, 1 tablespoon at a time, until you have a stiff, glossy meringue. Whisk in the cornflour and vinegar, then put the mixture in the prepared tin and smooth the top with a spatula.

3 Bake for 15-20 minutes until set and lightly browned. Don't worry if it looks very puffy – it will sink back down as it cools.

4 Lay a sheet of baking paper on a work surface and scatter over the extra tablespoon of caster sugar. Turn the meringue out of the tin onto the sugared paper and set aside to cool.

5 Purée 50g of the strawberries in a mini food processor, or by pressing them through a sieve. Remove the baking paper from the meringue, then spread over the Greek yogurt. Scatter over the rest of the chopped strawberries and drizzle over some of the purée. Roll up from one of the long sides to enclose the filling, then put on a serving plate, seam side down. Dust with the icing sugar, then slice and serve drizzled with the rest of the purée.

LEMON POLENTA CAKE

Polenta is a popular ingredient in Italian and Middle-Eastern cakes, adding lots of flavour and texture.

SERVES 12

PREP TIME 15 minutes **COOK TIME** 1 hour

INGREDIENTS

2 lemons
150g low-fat spread
150g caster sugar
3 eggs
100g gluten-free self-raising flour
1 teaspoon gluten-free baking powder
50g polenta
1 tablespoon Demerara sugar

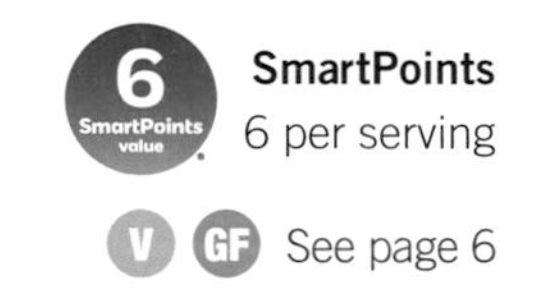

SmartPoints
6 per serving

See page 6

METHOD

1 Preheat the oven to 170°C, fan 150°C, gas mark 3½ and line a 900g loaf tin with baking paper.

2 Pare off a few long strips of lemon zest using a zester (or use a vegetable peeler to remove 2 strips of outer peel, then cut these into fine shreds), and set aside, covered, to finish the cake. Finely grate the rest of the zest from both lemons, and squeeze the juice from both.

3 In a large mixing bowl, beat the grated lemon zest, low-fat spread and caster sugar together using a hand-held electric whisk until pale and creamy. Beat in the eggs, one at a time, adding a spoonful of the flour with each egg. Add the rest of the flour, along with the baking powder, polenta and half the lemon juice. Mix for 1 minute until you have a smooth batter.

4 Pour the batter into the prepared tin, smooth the top with a spatula and bake for 40-60 minutes, or until a skewer inserted into the centre of the cake comes out clean.

5 Mix the remaining lemon juice with the Demerara sugar in a small jug. Pour over the top of the cake while it is still warm, then set aside to cool in the tin.

6 When the cake is cool, turn it out onto a serving plate and remove the baking paper. Top with the reserved pared lemon zest and cut into slices to serve.

STRAWBERRY BAKEWELL CAKE

An almond flavoured sponge is topped with fresh strawberries and flaked almonds.

SERVES 10

PREP TIME 15 minutes + cooling **COOK TIME** 50 minutes

INGREDIENTS

2 x 400g tins cannellini beans, drained and rinsed
8½ tablespoons agave syrup
100g low-fat spread
2 large eggs, plus 2 large egg whites
100g plain flour
2 teaspoons baking powder
1 teaspoon vanilla extract
1 teaspoon almond extract
175g fresh strawberries, hulled and halved
5g flaked almonds
1 teaspoon icing sugar

SmartPoints
5 per serving

METHOD

1 Preheat the oven to 180°C, fan 160°C, gas mark 4. Line the base and sides of a 20cm springform or loose-bottomed cake tin with baking paper.

2 Put the beans, agave syrup and spread in a food processor and blitz until smooth. Transfer to a large mixing bowl, whisk in the whole eggs, one at a time, then whisk in the egg whites.

3 Fold in the flour, baking powder and vanilla and almond extracts, then pour the mixture into the prepared tin. Arrange the strawberries, cut side up, on top and scatter over the flaked almonds.

4 Bake for 45-50 minutes or until a skewer inserted into the centre of the cake comes out clean. Leave to cool in the tin for 10 minutes, then carefully remove from the tin and transfer to a wire rack to cool completely. Dust with the icing sugar, then cut into slices and serve.

Tip

You can use any fresh berries you like on this cake. For a more traditional version, try cherries when in season.

BUTTERNUT SQUASH CAKE

This delicious loaf cake is flavoured with orange and fresh rosemary, and drizzled with orange icing.

SERVES 14

PREP TIME 20 minutes + cooling **COOK TIME** 2 hours

INGREDIENTS

125g low-fat spread, plus extra for greasing
½ butternut squash, seeds removed
Calorie controlled cooking spray
1 sprig fresh rosemary, leaves removed and finely chopped, plus an extra sprig to decorate
100g light brown soft sugar
3 large eggs
250g self-raising flour
Grated zest and juice of 1 orange
50g icing sugar

V 6 SmartPoints value

SmartPoints
6 per serving

METHOD

1 Preheat the oven to 200°C, fan 180°C, gas mark 6. Grease a 900g loaf tin with low-fat spread and line with baking paper. Put the butternut squash in a roasting tin and mist with cooking spray, then sprinkle over the chopped rosemary. Roast for 45 minutes, or until tender. Cool slightly, then scoop out 300g of the roasted flesh and purée with either a stick blender or potato masher.

2 In a large mixing bowl, beat together the low-fat spread and brown sugar using a hand-held electric whisk until light and fluffy. Beat in the eggs, one at a time, adding a spoonful of the flour with each egg. Gently fold the remaining flour, orange zest and butternut purée into the mixture.

3 Spoon the mixture into the prepared tin and bake for 1 hour 15 minutes, or until a skewer inserted into the centre of the cake comes out clean. Cover the cake with kitchen foil towards the end of cooking time if it is browning too much. Leave to cool in the tin for a few minutes, then turn out onto a wire rack to cool completely.

4 To decorate, mix the icing sugar with 2 teaspoons of the orange juice. Beat until smooth, adding a little more juice if needed. Drizzle over the top of the cake, decorate with the extra rosemary sprig, then slice and serve.

BANOFFEE WAFFLES

Waffles have never been so easy! These oat-based ones are baked, then topped with banana and toffee sauce.

MAKES 4

PREP TIME 15 minutes **COOK TIME** 35 minutes

INGREDIENTS

- Calorie controlled cooking spray
- 85g porridge oats
- 1 teaspoon baking powder
- 1 tablespoon cocoa powder
- 125ml skimmed milk
- 2 very ripe bananas, mashed and 2 just ripe bananas, sliced
- 1 large egg, lightly beaten
- 250g 0% fat natural Greek yogurt
- 4 tablespoons toffee sauce

YOU WILL ALSO NEED

Silicone waffle mould

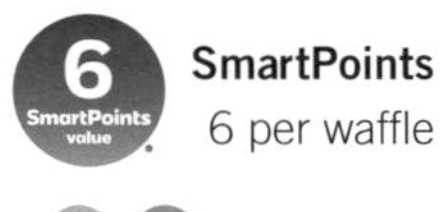

SmartPoints
6 per waffle

V GF See page 6

METHOD

1 Preheat the oven to 180°C, fan 160°C, gas mark 4. Mist a 4-hole silicone waffle mould with cooking spray and put on a baking sheet.

2 Combine the oats, baking powder, cocoa powder, milk, mashed bananas and egg in a bowl. Divide the mixture between the prepared moulds, then bake for 30-35 minutes until golden and a little crisp around the edges.

3 Carefully turn out the waffles onto plates. Top with the sliced bananas and yogurt, then drizzle 1 tablespoon toffee sauce over each waffle.

Tip

No waffle mould? You could also bake these in a 12-hole muffin tin, misted with cooking spray for 15-20 minutes.

BAKED VANILLA CHEESECAKE

Succulent fresh berries are the perfect accompaniment to this velvety-smooth baked cheesecake.

SERVES 10

PREP TIME 20 minutes + cooling **COOK TIME** 1 hour 5 minutes

INGREDIENTS

50g low-fat spread, melted, plus extra for greasing
125g Weight Watchers Ginger & Lemon Cookies
150g reduced-fat cottage cheese
300g low-fat soft cheese
170g low-fat vanilla yogurt
3 eggs
1 teaspoon vanilla extract
40g caster sugar
125g strawberries, hulled and halved
75g raspberries
75g blueberries

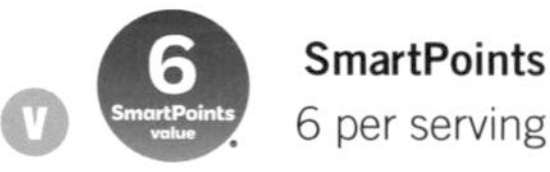

SmartPoints
6 per serving

METHOD

1 Preheat the oven to 180°C, fan 160°C, gas mark 4. Grease and line the base of an 18cm springform cake tin with baking paper.

2 Put the cookies in a food processor and blitz to a fine crumb, or put them in a sealed plastic food bag and crush with a rolling pin. Transfer to a mixing bowl and stir in the melted spread until well combined. Press the mixture evenly into the base of the prepared tin. Bake for 15 minutes, then remove from the oven and reduce the temperature to 150°C, fan 130°C, gas mark 2.

3 Press the cottage cheese through a sieve and put into a food processor. Add the soft cheese, yogurt, eggs, vanilla and sugar and blitz until smooth. Pour the mixture over the cookie base and shake the tin gently to level the surface.

4 Bake for 45-50 minutes until the cheesecake is set in the centre, but still slightly wobbly. Turn off the oven and leave the cheesecake in the oven as it cools, for at least 1 hour – this gradual cooling helps stop the cheesecake from cracking.

5 Chill until ready to serve, then carefully remove the cheesecake from the tin and pile the berries on top – you can serve any leftover berries on the side.

APPLE & SULTANA CAKE

A simple, fruity traybake that's sweetened with honey and flavoured with mixed spice.

SERVES 12

PREP TIME 15 minutes + cooling **COOK TIME** 35 minutes

INGREDIENTS

Low-fat spread for greasing
4 large eggs
4 tablespoons honey
75g low-fat natural yogurt
200g self-raising flour
1 teaspoon mixed spice
50g sultanas
2 large red apples, cored and thinly sliced
1 teaspoon agave syrup

SmartPoints
4 per serving

METHOD

1 Preheat the oven to 180°C, fan 160°C, gas mark 4. Grease a 20cm square tin with low-fat spread and line with baking paper.

2 In a large bowl, whisk together the eggs, honey and yogurt. Gently fold in the flour and mixed spice until all of the ingredients are combined and you have a smooth batter. Stir in the sultanas and most of the apple slices, reserving about 15 for decoration.

3 Pour the mixture into the prepared tin and smooth the top with a spatula. Top with the reserved apple slices, then bake for 30-35 minutes, or until the top is golden brown and a skewer inserted into the centre of the cake comes out clean.

4 Remove from the oven and brush over the agave syrup. Leave to cool for 10 minutes, then turn out onto a wire rack to cool completely. Remove the baking paper, then cut into 12 equal squares to serve.

BANANA CAKE

A lunchbox favourite, this is a great way to use up any overripe bananas in your fruit bowl.

SERVES 10

PREP TIME 20 minutes + cooling **COOK TIME** 1 hour 15 minutes

INGREDIENTS

Calorie controlled cooking spray
3-4 really ripe bananas (you'll need 300g peeled weight)
2 tablespoons clear honey
3 large eggs
150g 0% fat natural yogurt
2 teaspoons vanilla extract
150g porridge oats
100g plain flour
1 teaspoon baking powder

SmartPoints
3 per serving

METHOD

1 Preheat the oven to 160°C, fan 140°C, gas mark 3. Mist a 900g loaf tin with cooking spray and line the base and ends with a long strip of overhanging baking paper.

2 Put the bananas, honey, eggs, yogurt and vanilla in a food processor and blitz until smooth. Transfer to a large mixing bowl. Wipe the bowl of the food processor clean.

3 Reserve 2 teaspoons of the oats and put the rest in the food processor with the flour and baking powder, then blitz to a fine flour. Add to the banana mixture and stir to combine. Pour the mixture into the prepared tin. Scatter over the reserved oats and bake for 1 hour to 1 hour 15 minutes, until a skewer inserted into the centre of the loaf comes out clean, with just a few sticky crumbs.

4 Leave to cool in the tin, then turn out and slice to serve.

VANILLA CAKE WITH MERINGUE KISSES

This makes a great celebration cake for a birthday, or any other special occasion.

SERVES 12

PREP TIME 30 minutes + cooling **COOK TIME** 1 hour 20 minutes

INGREDIENTS

Calorie controlled cooking spray
175g self-raising flour
½ tablespoon baking powder
150g caster sugar
150g low-fat spread
3 eggs
½ tablespoon vanilla extract

FOR THE MERINGUE KISSES

1 egg white
60g caster sugar
½ teaspoon red gel food colouring

TO FILL AND DECORATE

4 teaspoons low-calorie raspberry jam
150g strawberries, hulled and sliced
75g raspberries

YOU WILL ALSO NEED

Piping bag

SmartPoints
8 per serving

Serve without the meringues for **6 SmartPoints** per serving

METHOD

1 Preheat the oven to 180°C, fan 160°C, gas mark 4. Mist two 18cm sandwich tins with cooking spray and line with baking paper.

2 Sift the flour and baking powder into a mixing bowl and add the sugar, low-fat spread, eggs and vanilla extract. Beat for 3 minutes or until pale and creamy, then divide between the tins and smooth with a spatula. Bake for 15-18 minutes until the sponges are risen, golden and springy to the touch. Set aside to cool in their tins for 5 minutes, then turn out onto a wire rack, remove the baking paper and leave to cool completely.

3 To make the meringue kisses, reduce the oven temperature to 120°C, fan 100°C, gas mark ½. Line a baking sheet with baking paper. Using a hand-held electric whisk, whisk the egg white in a mixing bowl until it forms stiff peaks that hold their shape when the beaters are removed. Gradually whisk in the sugar until the mixture is smooth, stiff and glossy.

4 Drizzle the food colouring in 3 lines down the inside of a piping bag fitted with a 1.5cm nozzle, then add the meringue mixture. Pipe blobs of the meringue onto the prepared baking sheet, lifting the piping bag up sharply at the end to create points. Bake for 45-60 minutes until crisp and dry. Turn off the oven and leave the meringues in the oven with the door closed until completely cool.

5 Put one of the sponges upside down on a serving plate and spread over the jam. Arrange two-thirds of the strawberries over the jam, then top with the other sponge. Pile the rest of the strawberries, raspberries and meringue kisses on top of the cake and serve with any leftover meringues on the side.

Bread, scones & muffins

RICOTTA CHEESE SCONES

These savoury scones are flavoured with chives and black pepper, then sprinkled with grated cheese.

MAKES 12

PREP TIME 20 minutes **COOK TIME** 12 minutes

INGREDIENTS

320g self-raising flour, plus extra for dusting
½ teaspoon baking powder
120g ricotta cheese
40g vegetarian hard Italian-style cheese, finely grated
2 eggs
1 teaspoon ground black pepper
2 teaspoons mustard powder
1 tablespoon chopped fresh chives
Pinch of salt
150ml skimmed milk

SmartPoints
4 per scone

METHOD

1 Preheat the oven to 220°C, fan 200°C, gas mark 7. Line a baking sheet with baking paper.

2 Put the flour and baking powder in a large mixing bowl. In a separate bowl beat together the ricotta, half the grated hard cheese, 1 of the eggs, the pepper, mustard powder, chives and a pinch of salt. Add the wet ingredients to the dry and mix well with just enough of the milk to form a soft dough.

3 Dust a work surface with the extra flour, turn out the dough and knead for 3 minutes. Roll out the dough to a thickness of 3cm, then cut out 12 rounds with a 6cm pastry cutter – you will need to reroll the trimmings.

4 Beat the remaining egg in a small bowl. Put the scones on the prepared baking sheet, leaving room for them to expand, and brush the tops with the beaten egg. Sprinkle over the remaining grated hard cheese and bake for 10-12 minutes or until risen and golden.

SWEET POTATO MUFFINS

These flourless muffins use sweet potato and ground almonds, to make them gluten free.

MAKES 8

PREP TIME 20 minutes + cooling **COOK TIME** 35 minutes

FOR THE MUFFINS
150g sweet potato, peeled and cut into 2cm cubes
2 eggs, lightly beaten
2 tablespoons vegetable oil
4 tablespoons maple syrup
60g ground almonds
2 teaspoons baking powder
1 teaspoon ground cinnamon

FOR THE FROSTING
150g 0% fat natural Greek yogurt
1 tablespoons maple syrup
15g pecan halves, toasted and roughly chopped

SmartPoints
5 per muffin

V GF See page 6

METHOD

1 Preheat the oven to 180°C, fan 160°C, gas mark 4. Line 8 holes of a 12-hole muffin tin with paper cases.

2 Put the sweet potatoes in a microwave-safe bowl with 3 tablespoons water. Cover with clingfilm, pierce several holes in it and cook for 10-12 minutes on high until tender. Drain the cooked sweet potato, transfer to a mini food processor and blitz until smooth, or put in a bowl and mash using a potato masher.

3 In a mixing bowl, beat together the eggs, vegetable oil and maple syrup using a hand-held electric whisk until light and frothy. Fold in the almonds, baking powder, cinnamon and the cooled sweet potato until you have a smooth batter. Spoon the mixture into the paper cases.

4 Bake for 15-20 minutes or until firm to the touch. Remove from the oven, transfer to a wire rack and set aside to cool completely.

5 To make the frosting, in a small bowl, fold the yogurt and the maple syrup together. Spoon on top of the muffins, scatter over the chopped pecans, then serve.

SAVOURY BREAKFAST MUFFINS

These savoury bakes are packed full of flavour and great for breakfast on the go.

MAKES 9

PREP TIME 20 minutes **COOK TIME** 35 minutes

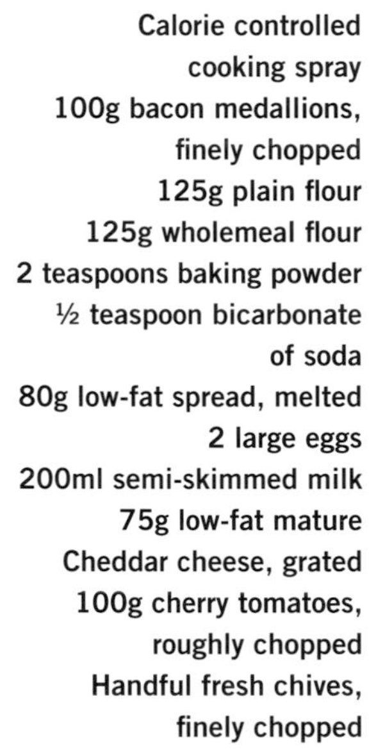

INGREDIENTS

Calorie controlled cooking spray
100g bacon medallions, finely chopped
125g plain flour
125g wholemeal flour
2 teaspoons baking powder
½ teaspoon bicarbonate of soda
80g low-fat spread, melted
2 large eggs
200ml semi-skimmed milk
75g low-fat mature Cheddar cheese, grated
100g cherry tomatoes, roughly chopped
Handful fresh chives, finely chopped

SmartPoints
5 per muffin

METHOD

1 Preheat the oven to 190°C, fan 170°C, gas mark 5. Line 9 holes of a 12-hole muffin tin with paper cases.

2 Mist a frying pan with cooking spray and put over a medium heat. Fry the bacon for 2-3 minutes, turning occasionally, until golden, then remove from the heat and set aside.

3 In a large bowl, combine the flours, baking powder and bicarbonate of soda, then season.

4 In a separate bowl, beat together the cooled melted spread, eggs, milk and cheese and add to the dry ingredients. Mix well, then stir in the bacon, tomatoes and chives until combined.

5 Divide the mixture between the muffin cases and bake for 25-30 minutes, or until risen and golden.

CHOCOLATE MUFFINS

These tempting muffins couldn't be simpler. Top with more chocolate, if you like, for an extra treat!

MAKES 6

PREP TIME 5 minutes + cooling **COOK TIME** 20 minutes

INGREDIENTS

3 large very ripe bananas (about 450g peeled weight)
4 eggs, lightly beaten
4 tablespoons cocoa powder
20g dark chocolate, to decorate

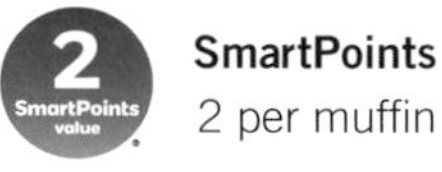

SmartPoints
2 per muffin

V GF See page 6

METHOD

1 Preheat the oven to 180°C, fan 160°C, gas mark 4. Line 6 holes of a muffin tin with paper cases.

2 Put the bananas, eggs and cocoa powder in a food processor or blender and blitz until completely smooth. Divide the mixture between the paper cases and bake for 15-20 minutes or until a skewer inserted in the centre of a muffin comes out clean.

3 Transfer to a wire rack to cool completely. Put the chocolate in a microwave-safe bowl and microwave on high for 30 seconds or until melted. Drizzle the melted chocolate over the muffins, then allow to set before serving.

Tip

If you prefer to leave off the chocolate topping, these are only 1 SmartPoint each.

EARL GREY SCONES

These tea-flavoured scones are served with a delicious blueberry compote and Greek yogurt.

MAKES 12

PREP TIME 20 minutes + resting **COOK TIME** 15 minutes

INGREDIENTS

150ml skimmed milk
3 Earl Grey tea bags
375g plain flour, plus extra for dusting
20g baking powder
75g low-fat spread
50g caster sugar
3 eggs
Grated zest of 1 lemon
150ml 0% fat natural Greek yogurt, to serve

FOR THE BLUEBERRY COMPOTE

500g blueberries
1 tablespoon cornflour, mixed with a splash of water
1 teaspoon vanilla extract

SmartPoints
5 per scone

METHOD

1 Put the milk in a pan and bring to a simmer. Add the tea bags, remove from the heat and leave to steep until the milk has cooled to room temperature, then discard the tea bags.

2 Put the flour, baking powder and spread in a large mixing bowl and use your fingertips to rub together until the mixture resembles breadcrumbs. Stir in the sugar.

3 In a separate bowl, whisk 2 of the eggs with the cooled infused milk, then add to the mixing bowl along with the lemon zest. Stir to form a sticky dough.

4 Line a baking sheet with baking paper. Dust a work surface with flour and knead the dough for 3-5 minutes. Roll out to a thickness of 3cm and cut out 12 rounds using a 6cm cutter – you will need to reroll the trimmings. Put the scones on the prepared baking sheet, leaving room for them to expand. Rest at room temperature for 45 minutes to 1 hour.

5 Preheat the oven to 220°C, fan 200°C, gas mark 7. Beat the remaining egg in a small bowl and brush over the scones. Bake for 15 minutes or until risen and golden.

6 Meanwhile, put the blueberries in a small pan over a medium heat. Cook for 7 minutes or until the blueberries are beginning to split and release their juice. Stir in the cornflour paste and cook for 3 minutes until thickened. Stir in the vanilla extract and set aside to cool. Serve the scones topped with the blueberry compote and the Greek yogurt.

CHOCOLATE BREAD & BUTTER PUDDING

This chocolate version of the traditional dessert makes the perfect warming pud.

SERVES 6

PREP TIME 15 minutes **COOK TIME** 35 minutes

INGREDIENTS

9 slices Weight Watchers Malted Danish bread, lightly toasted
25g low-fat spread
3 large eggs
3 tablespoons light hot chocolate powder
1 tablespoon cocoa powder
2 teaspoons agave syrup
1 teaspoon vanilla extract
200ml unsweetened almond milk
25g dark chocolate chips

SmartPoints
6 per serving

METHOD

1 Preheat the oven to 160°C, fan 140°C, gas mark 3. Spread each slice of toast with a little of the spread and cut in half diagonally.

2 Whisk together the eggs, hot chocolate powder, cocoa powder, agave syrup, vanilla and almond milk in a jug until smooth.

3 Arrange the toast in a small baking dish then pour over the chocolate custard mixture and leave to soak for 5 minutes.

4 Scatter over the chocolate chips then bake for 30-35 minutes until cooked through. Serve warm.

MIXED BERRY BREAD

This soft, brioche-style loaf filled with mixed berries, makes for a great sweet breakfast.

SERVES 15

PREP TIME 25 minutes + proving & cooling **COOK TIME** 45 minutes

INGREDIENTS

100ml semi-skimmed milk
350g strong white bread flour, plus extra for dusting
1 teaspoon salt
7g sachet fast action dried yeast
4 eggs
60g low-fat spread
Calorie controlled cooking spray
3 tablespoons low-calorie blackberry jam
100g frozen mixed berries

SmartPoints
3 per serving

METHOD

1 Gently warm the milk in a small pan over a low heat until it's warm to the touch, but not hot.

2 Put the flour, salt and yeast in the bowl of a free-standing mixer fitted with a dough hook. Turn the mixer on for 30 seconds to combine the dry ingredients. Add the warmed milk and 3 of the eggs, and mix on a low speed for 2 minutes, then increase the speed and mix for a further 8 minutes. Gradually add spoonfuls of the low-fat spread, mixing for a further 5 minutes and scraping the dough down from the sides of the bowl as you go. The dough should feel soft but not sticky. If you don't have a free-standing mixer, mix and knead the dough by hand until it is smooth and elastic, then knead in the spread, bit by bit.

3 Put the dough in a bowl misted with cooking spray and cover with misted clingfilm. Leave in a warm place (not too warm as you don't want the dough to become too soft) for 1-2 hours, or until doubled in size. If it starts to get too warm and soft, transfer it to the fridge to firm up a little.

4 When the dough has doubled in size, turn it out onto a lightly floured work surface and knock out the air, then press out into a rough rectangle about the same length as a 900g nonstick loaf tin. Spread over the jam and scatter over the berries, then roll up the dough and put in the loaf tin. Loosely cover with oiled clingfilm and leave to prove for 30 minutes or until slightly risen.

5 Preheat the oven to 200°C, fan 180°C, gas mark 6. Beat the remaining egg in a small bowl and brush over the top of the loaf. Bake for 35-40 minutes or until golden brown. Leave to cool in the tin for 10 minutes, then transfer to a wire rack to cool completely.

MUSIC PAPER BREAD

These paper-thin flatbreads originated in Sardinia – try serving them with a salad, dip or fresh tomato salsa.

MAKES 8

PREP TIME 10 minutes + resting **COOK TIME** 25 minutes

INGREDIENTS

150g 00 grade pasta flour, plus extra for dusting
75g fine semolina
3 tablespoons olive oil
1 teaspoon sea salt
3 sprigs fresh rosemary, leaves picked and roughly chopped

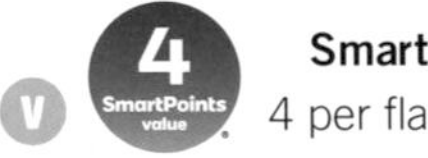

SmartPoints
4 per flatbread

METHOD

1 In a bowl, combine the flour and semolina. Mix in 150ml water to form a soft dough. Transfer to a lightly floured surface and knead for around 5 minutes or until smooth. Use a little of the oil to grease the bowl. Return the dough to the bowl, cover and set aside to rest for 1 hour.

2 Preheat the oven to the highest setting it will reach – typically 240°C, fan 220°C, gas mark 9. Put 2 large baking sheets in the oven to heat up.

3 Tear off 8 pieces of baking paper, each one about 30cm long. Divide the dough into 8 and roll out each piece to a rough circle, about 20cm in diameter. Put each circle onto a piece of baking paper, drizzle with the remaining olive oil, then scatter over the sea salt and rosemary. Slide a piece of the dough (still on the baking paper) onto each baking tray and cook for 5-6 minutes, or until crisp and golden brown. Put on a wire rack to cool as you cook the remaining pieces of bread.

SODA BREAD

This uses bicarbonate of soda instead of yeast, making it a speedy bread recipe.

SERVES 14

PREP TIME 10 minutes + cooling **COOK TIME** 30 minutes

INGREDIENTS

200g self-raising wholemeal flour, plus extra for dusting
200g plain flour
½ teaspoon bicarbonate of soda
60g jumbo oats
1 teaspoon salt
1 tablespoon dark brown soft sugar
350ml buttermilk
Calorie controlled cooking spray

SmartPoints
4 per serving

METHOD

1 Preheat the oven to 220°C, fan 200°C, gas mark 7. Put a medium casserole dish with the lid on in the oven to heat while you prepare the dough.

2 Sift both flours and the bicarbonate of soda into a large mixing bowl and add in any bran that's left behind in the sieve. Add 50g of the oats, the salt and sugar, then stir through the buttermilk to form a sticky dough.

3 Turn out onto a lightly floured surface and form into a large round loaf. Dip the handle of a wooden spoon into some flour and use it to gently press a cross into the top of the loaf.

4 Remove the heated casserole dish from the oven and mist with cooking spray, then transfer the dough to the casserole. Scatter over the remaining oats, then cover with the lid and bake for 25-30 minutes or until the loaf is risen and golden. Leave for 15 minutes in the casserole dish, then transfer to a wire rack to cool completely.

PIZZA LOAF

A tasty filled loaf that's great on its own, or delicious served alongside a bowl of your favourite soup.

SERVES 12

PREP TIME 45 minutes + proving & cooling **COOK TIME** 40 minutes

INGREDIENTS

250g strong white bread flour, plus extra for dusting
1 teaspoon salt
½ teaspoon caster sugar
3g fast-action dried yeast
1½ tablespoons olive oil, plus extra for greasing
50g pitted green olives, roughly chopped
70g sun-dried tomatoes in oil, drained and roughly chopped
Small handful fresh basil, roughly chopped
125g light mozzarella, torn into small chunks
1 egg, lightly beaten

SmartPoints
4 per serving

METHOD

1 Sift the flour into a large mixing bowl and add the salt, sugar and yeast. Make a well in the centre, then pour in 120ml warm water and the oil, and mix with a wooden spoon to form a soft dough. Add a little extra warm water if the dough is too dry.

2 Turn the dough out onto a lightly floured work surface and knead for 7-10 minutes, or until it is smooth and elastic. Transfer to a lightly oiled bowl, cover with a tea towel and leave in a warm place for 1 hour or until doubled in size.

3 Meanwhile, combine the green olives with the sun-dried tomatoes, basil and some freshly ground black pepper.

4 Turn the dough out onto a lightly floured work surface. Knock out the air by punching the dough and stretching it back and forth for a few minutes. Roll into a 36cm x 22cm rectangle. Spread over the tomato and olive mixture and dot with pieces of the mozzarella. Starting from the longest edge, roll the dough tightly into a sausage shape. Cut in half lengthways, but leave 3cm uncut at one end so the two halves are still attached. Twist the two halves together like a rope.

5 Put the dough on a large baking sheet lined with baking paper. Cover with a lightly oiled piece of clingfilm and set aside in a warm place to prove for a further 35 minutes.

6 Preheat the oven to 220°C, fan 200°C, gas mark 7. Brush the loaf with the beaten egg and bake for 35-40 minutes or until cooked through and golden. If the loaf is catching on top, cover loosely with foil. Allow to cool for 5 minutes, then slice and serve warm.

GARLIC DOUGH BALLS

These soft, tear-and-share mini rolls are great served warm with pasta dishes, soups or salads.

MAKES 12

PREP TIME 30 minutes + proving & cooling **COOK TIME** 15 minutes

INGREDIENTS

- **250g strong white bread flour, plus extra for dusting**
- **1 teaspoon caster sugar**
- **½ teaspoon salt**
- **1 teaspoon garlic granules**
- **½ teaspoon fast action dried yeast**
- **Calorie controlled cooking spray**
- **1½ tablespoons low-fat spread**
- **1 garlic clove, crushed**
- **1 tablespoon fresh flat-leaf parsley, finely chopped**

SmartPoints
2 per roll

METHOD

1 Put the flour, sugar, salt and garlic granules into a large mixing bowl. Stir through the yeast and make a well in the centre. Pour 150ml warm water into the well and stir everything together to form a soft dough. Turn out onto a lightly floured surface and knead for 5-7 minutes or until smooth and springy.

2 Mist a large baking sheet with cooking spray. Divide the dough into 12 equal pieces, roll into balls and arrange them on the baking sheet, so they're almost touching. Cover with misted clingfilm and leave in a warm place for 35 minutes, or until doubled in size.

3 Preheat the oven to 220°C, fan 200°C, gas mark 7. In a small bowl, mash together the spread, garlic and parsley. Set aside.

4 Remove the clingfilm from the risen dough and bake for 15 minutes or until golden. Set aside to cool for 5 minutes, then brush with the garlic butter to serve.

GLUTEN-FREE HERBY FOCACCIA

This Italian-style bread is sprinkled with sea salt, drizzled with olive oil and topped with fresh herbs.

SERVES 16

PREP TIME 20 minutes + proving **COOK TIME** 30 minutes

INGREDIENTS

200ml semi-skimmed milk
2 eggs
4½ tablespoons olive oil
1 tablespoon clear honey
400g gluten-free white bread flour
7g sachet dried yeast
1½ teaspoons xanthan gum
2 teaspoons cider vinegar
¼ teaspoon bicarbonate of soda
3 sprigs fresh rosemary
3 sprigs fresh thyme, cut into smaller sprigs
1 tablespoon sea salt

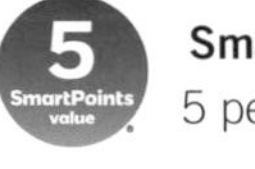

SmartPoints
5 per serving

V GF See page 6

METHOD

1 Preheat the oven to 200°C, fan 180°C, gas mark 6. Gently heat the milk in a small pan over a low heat, until it's warm to the touch, but not hot. Put the eggs, 2 tablespoons of the oil and the honey into a bowl, and whisk in the warmed milk.

2 In a large mixing bowl, combine the flour, yeast and xanthan gum, and make a well in the centre. Pour the milk mixture into the well and stir everything together to form a sticky dough.

3 In a small jug, combine the vinegar with the bicarbonate of soda and immediately add it to the dough, mixing thoroughly. Grease a baking sheet with ½ tablespoon of the oil and, using wet fingers, stretch and smooth the dough onto the baking sheet right up into the corners. Cover with lightly oiled clingfilm and leave in a warm place for 1½ hours, or until doubled in size.

4 Once risen, use the end of a wooden spoon, dipped in gluten-free flour, to make random holes in the dough. Poke small sprigs of the herbs in each hole, drizzle the entire loaf with the remaining 2 tablespoons of olive oil and sprinkle over the sea salt. Bake for 25-30 minutes or until golden and cooked through. Serve warm.

Tip

You can find xanthan gum in most supermarkets. It helps give this gluten-free bread a spongy, chewy texture.

Recipe index

SmartPoints index

weight watchers SmartPoints